AUTO RACING SUPER STATS

JEFF SAVAGE

Lerner Publications ◆ Minneapolis

Statistics are through November 2016, the end of the NASCAR Cup Series season, unless otherwise noted.

Lerner Publications Company
A division of Lerner Publishing Group, Inc.
241 First Avenue North
Minneapolis, MN 55401 USA

For reading levels and more information, look up this title at www.lernerbooks.com.

Main body text set in Aptifer Sans LT Pro 12/18.
Typeface provided by Linotype AG.

Library of Congress Cataloging-in-Publication Data

Names: Savage, Jeff, 1961– author.
Title: Auto Racing Super Stats / Jeff Savage.
Description: Minneapolis, MN : Lerner Publications, 2017. | Series: Pro Sports Stats |
    Includes bibliographical references and index. | Audience: Age 8–12. | Audience:
    Grade 4 to 6.
Identifiers: LCCN 2016052487 (print) | LCCN 2016055913 (ebook) | ISBN
    9781512434125 (lb : alk. paper) | ISBN 9781512449433 (eb pdf)
Subjects: LCSH: Stock car racing—United States—Biography—Juvenile literature.
    | Stock car drivers—United States—Biography—Juvenile literature. | NASCAR
    (Association)—Juvenile literature.
Classification: LCC GV1029.9.S74 S28 2017 (print) | LCC GV1029.9.S74 (ebook) | DDC
    796.720922 [B] —dc23

LC record available at https://lccn.loc.gov/2016052487

Manufactured in the United States of America
1-42048-23918-1/24/2017

TABLE OF CONTENTS

WORLD OF RACING

Auto racing is the world's fastest sport. Drivers propel their cars at incredible speeds on tracks all around the world. How do fans and racing teams (the drivers, mechanics, and others who make race cars go) keep up with it all? They study statistics (stats)! What are auto racing's most important stats? First, it's helpful to know about different types of popular auto races.

NASCAR

The National Association for Stock Car Auto Racing (NASCAR) began competing in 1949. It is second in sports to the National Football League (NFL) in the number of fans and television viewers in the United States. Since 2001, 36 **Cup Series** races are held each year. Most NASCAR tracks are shaped like ovals, but each track is unique.

A 2016 CUP SERIES RACE

DRAG RACING

This is racing in which two cars line up side by side and roar down a straight track to the finish line. The National Hot Rod Association (NHRA) holds the most popular drag races in the United States, including the fastest professional classes of drag racing: Top Fuel and Funny Car.

FORMULA ONE

Formula One (F1) is the world's most popular auto racing series. A formula is a set of rules that car designers must follow. These **open-wheel** race cars are built to make sharp turns at high speeds. A series of races, called Grands Prix (French for "grand prizes"), are held on twisty courses that often include city streets. About half the races are in Europe.

INDYCAR

This series of races is the United States version of open-wheel racing. The name comes from one of the country's most famous

INDYCAR

races, the Indianapolis 500. The race debuted in 1911. The IndyCar series features races on oval tracks as well as **road courses**.

CHAPTER ONE

DRIVER SUPER STATS

HOT WHEELS!

Sometimes a racing team can fine-tune a car so perfectly that it's nearly impossible to beat. In 1967 the great Richard Petty's Plymouth Belvedere GTX was fast on any type of NASCAR course—**dirt tracks**, **short tracks**, and **speedways**. The car helped the legendary driver win more races in a row than anyone in NASCAR history.

RICHARD PETTY

Most NASCAR Wins in a Row

DRIVER	WINS IN A ROW	YEAR
Richard Petty	10	1967
Richard Petty	6	1971
Bobby Allison	5	1971
Jimmie Johnson	4	2007
Jeff Gordon	4	1998
Mark Martin	4	1993
Bill Elliott	4	1992
Harry Gant	4	1991
Dale Earnhardt	4	1987
Darrell Waltrip	4	1981
Cale Yarborough	4	1976
David Pearson	4	1968
David Pearson	4	1966
Billy Wade	4	1964

TAKING THE CHECKERED FLAG

The great Richard Petty sped around NASCAR tracks from the 1960s to the 1990s. He is the all-time runaway leader in races won for NASCAR's top racing series. But Petty had more chances to enter **victory lane** than racers who began their NASCAR careers later. From 1956 to 1965, there were more than 50 races most years, with a high of 62 races in 1964. Since 2001 the series has had exactly 36 races each year.

HISTORY HIGHLIGHT

Richard Petty was called the King. He comes from a family of race car drivers. His father, Lee, won the first Daytona 500, NASCAR's most famous race. In 1959 in Lakewood, Georgia, Richard Petty won his first race—or so he thought. His father complained about an error, saying his son hadn't driven enough laps. The laps were checked, and Lee Petty was awarded the victory instead. Richard Petty won his first race a year later—and 200 in his career.

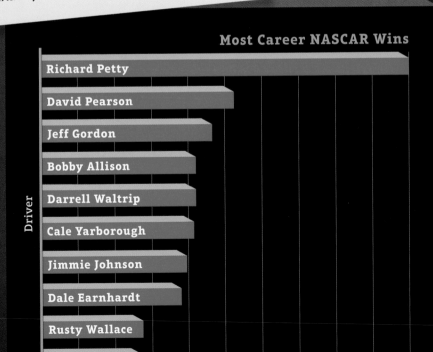

Most Career NASCAR Wins

Driver

Richard Petty
David Pearson
Jeff Gordon
Bobby Allison
Darrell Waltrip
Cale Yarborough
Jimmie Johnson
Dale Earnhardt
Rusty Wallace

JIMMIE JOHNSON

21ST CENTURY GREATS

Since 2001, when the NASCAR schedule changed to 36 events, the races have been staged on a variety of courses. There are short tracks, **medium tracks**, speedways, and road courses. Many of the courses host more than one event. The best drivers and cars are able to win on any type of track.

Most NASCAR Cup Series Wins since 2001

Driver

- Jimmie Johnson
- Jeff Gordon
- Tony Stewart
- Kyle Busch
- Matt Kenseth
- Kevin Harvick
- Denny Hamlin
- Kurt Busch
- Carl Edwards
- Dale Earnhardt Jr.

THE NEW GENERATION

Generation-6 (Gen 6) **stock cars** were introduced for the NASCAR Cup Series in 2013. The cars have bars in the roof to prevent the car from being crushed in a crash. But with lighter parts in other places, Gen 6 models still weigh 160 pounds (73 kilograms) less than Gen 5 cars. Gen 6 cars also look more like cars you might see on the street than previous generations. Note that since 2013, about 40 cars have competed in each NASCAR race.

GEN 6 STOCK CAR

Best Drivers in Gen 6 Cars

DRIVER	TOTAL RACES	AVERAGE POSITION AT END OF RACE
Kevin Harvick	144	10.7
Joey Logano	144	11.3
Brad Keselowski	144	12.5
Dale Earnhardt Jr.	126	12.6
Jeff Gordon	116	12.9
Jimmie Johnson	144	13.2
Kyle Busch	133	13.3
Matt Kenseth	142	13.3
Carl Edwards	144	14.1
Denny Hamlin	139	14.9

REPEAT CHAMPIONS

A popular statistic among NASCAR fans is yearly champion. How a driver does against some of the best racers in the world is a true measure of ability, no matter the era. Points are awarded for each race in a season based on a driver's finish. Richard Petty won seven championships. He also finished second in the season-long competition six times!

HISTORY HIGHLIGHT

Dale Earnhardt was a fan favorite. He joined NASCAR in 1975 and soon earned a reputation as an aggressive driver. His nickname was the Intimidator. Earnhardt won 76 Cup Series races and seven championships, tied for most all time. He struggled to win the Daytona 500, but finally, in his 20th attempt, he captured the crown at Daytona International Speedway. Three years later, he was killed there in a crash.

DALE EARNHARDT

Most NASCAR Championships

DRIVER	CHAMPIONSHIPS	YEARS
Dale Earnhardt	7	1980, 1986, 1987, 1990, 1991, 1993, 1994
Jimmie Johnson	7	2006, 2007, 2008, 2009, 2010, 2013, 2016
Richard Petty	7	1964, 1967, 1971, 1972, 1974, 1975, 1979
Jeff Gordon	4	1995, 1997, 1998, 2001
David Pearson	3	1966, 1968, 1969
Lee Petty	3	1954, 1958, 1959
Tony Stewart	3	2002, 2005, 2011
Darrell Waltrip	3	1981, 1982, 1985
Cale Yarborough	3	1976, 1977, 1978

2016 INDIANAPOLIS 500

THE BRICKYARD

Indianapolis Motor Speedway in Speedway, Indiana, is also known as the Brickyard. It is the site of one of IndyCar's most popular races— the Indianapolis 500. The Indy 500 is called the Greatest Spectacle in Racing by fans, and about 300,000 people attend the event each Memorial Day weekend. Drivers race 200 laps around a 2.5-mile (4-kilometer) oval, for a total distance of 500 miles (805 km). The winner is awarded more than $2.5 million.

Most Indianapolis 500 Wins

DRIVER	WINS	YEARS
A. J. Foyt	4	1961, 1964, 1967, 1977
Rick Mears	4	1979, 1984, 1988, 1991
Al Unser	4	1970, 1971, 1978, 1987
Helio Castroneves	3	2001, 2002, 2009
Dario Franchitti	3	2007, 2010, 2012
Louis Meyer	3	1928, 1933, 1936
Mauri Rose	3	1941, 1947, 1948

WHOOSH!

IndyCars can go *really* fast. During a **qualifying lap**, an IndyCar driver may push the average speed to 230 miles (370 km) per hour or more. But during races, it's all too easy to smash up the expensive vehicles with other cars crowding the track. The average speed of the winning car at the 2016 Indianapolis 500 was just under 167 miles (269 km) per hour. Winning an IndyCar race takes a lot more than pure speed. It takes the skill to avoid trouble and a little bit of luck too.

IndyCar All-Time Wins

Driver

- A. J. Foyt
- Mario Andretti
- Michael Andretti
- Scott Dixon
- Al Unser
- Bobby Unser
- Al Unser Jr.
- Sebastien Bourdais
- Paul Tracy
- Dario Franchitti
- Helio Castroneves
- Rick Mears

WINNING TAKES WILL POWER

Driver Will Power raced in Australia and Europe before racing full-time in the United States beginning in 2008. The other drivers in the IndyCar series wish he'd stayed overseas. Since 2010 famous drivers such as Marco Andretti, Takuma Sato, and Charlie Kimball have won just one race each. That's partly because Power wins more than one out of every five races he enters.

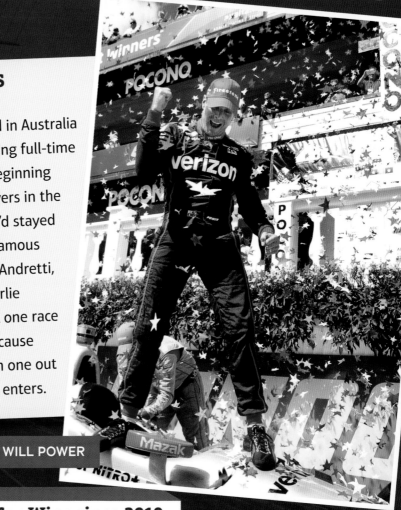

WILL POWER

Most IndyCar Wins since 2010

DRIVER	WINS
Will Power	25
Scott Dixon	18
Ryan Hunter-Reay	13
Simon Pagenaud	9
Dario Franchitti	8
Helio Castroneves	7
Sebastien Bourdais	4
Mike Conway	4
James Hinchcliffe	4
Juan Pablo Montoya	4

STATS FACT

Danica Patrick's victory in the 2008 Indy Japan 300 is the only IndyCar win by a woman at the top level. She finished third in the 2009 Indianapolis 500. In 2013 she switched to NASCAR.

THE RIGHT FORMULA

The Formula One World Championship started in 1950. Like in NASCAR, drivers collect points for each race to determine the yearly champion. Michael Schumacher holds nearly every career F1 record. He won seven championships, including five in a row from 2000 to 2004 while driving a Ferrari. In the 2002 season, he became the only driver ever to finish in the top three in every race.

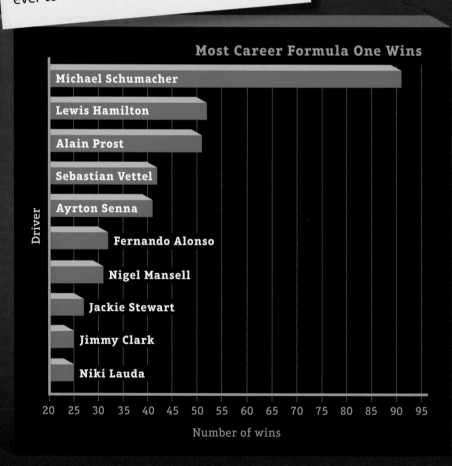

Most Career Formula One Wins

Driver (vertical axis):
Michael Schumacher
Lewis Hamilton
Alain Prost
Sebastian Vettel
Ayrton Senna
Fernando Alonso
Nigel Mansell
Jackie Stewart
Jimmy Clark
Niki Lauda

Number of wins (horizontal axis): 20 25 30 35 40 45 50 55 60 65 70 75 80 85 90 95

THE GRAND PRIZE OF MONACO

The Monaco Grand Prix is one of the most famous F1 races in the world. The narrow course winds through the streets of Monaco in western Europe and features sharp corners and a tunnel. Ayrton Senna won the race five straight years before dying in a crash in another Formula One race the following year.

MONACO GRAND PRIX

Most Monaco Grand Prix Wins

DRIVER	WINS	YEARS WON
Ayrton Senna	6	1987, 1989, 1990, 1991, 1992, 1993
Graham Hill	5	1963, 1964, 1965, 1968, 1969
Michael Schumacher	5	1994, 1995, 1997, 1999, 2001
Alain Prost	4	1984, 1985, 1986, 1988
Stirling Moss	3	1956, 1960, 1961
Nico Rosberg	3	2013, 2014, 2015
Jackie Stewart	3	1966, 1971, 1973

MISSILES ON WHEELS

At 25 feet (7.6 meters) long and less than 2 feet (0.6 m) wide at its nose, a Top Fuel drag racing car is shaped sort of like a missile. It cuts through the air like one too. Top Fuel cars travel a distance of more than three football fields in less than four seconds. Beginning in 2006, a yearly champion is determined in a playoff format involving several race events called Countdown to the Championship.

TOP FUEL

STATS FACT

In 1977 Shirley Muldowney became the first woman to win the NHRA Top Fuel points championship. She became the NHRA's first two-time winner in 1980 and the first three-time champion in 1982.

Top Fuel Champions since 2006

YEAR	DRIVER
2015	Antron Brown
2014	Tony Schumacher
2013	Shawn Langdon
2012	Antron Brown
2011	Del Worsham
2010	Larry Dixon
2009	Tony Schumacher
2008	Tony Schumacher
2007	Tony Schumacher
2006	Tony Schumacher

FUNNY CARS

Like Top Fuel cars, Funny Cars burn huge amounts of fuel to roar short distances as fast as possible. But unlike Top Fuel cars, which are long and sleek with the engine behind the driver, Funny Cars look similar to cars you'd see on the street. They're called Funny Cars because the rear wheels are larger and closer to the middle of the vehicle than on most cars. This makes them look funny.

Most Career Funny Car Wins

Driver

- John Force
- Ron Capps
- Tony Pedregon
- Robert Hight
- Don Prudhomme
- Cruz Pedregon
- Del Worsham
- Kenny Bernstein
- Jack Beckman
- Matt Hagan

CHAPTER TWO

CAR, TRACK, AND TEAM SUPER STATS

Some NASCAR tracks are faster than others. The way a track is set up—including its surface, curves, and **pit stops**—determines how fast a driver can go. The day before most races, drivers take turns speeding around the track on a qualifying lap. The fastest qualifying times guarantee drivers a spot in the race. How fast they go in qualifying also determines the order in which the cars will line up at the beginning of the race. The qualifying lap provides a true measure of the speed of a track. Drivers don't have to worry about other cars in their path, so they can zoom at top speeds.

Fastest Average Speed in a NASCAR Qualifying Lap since 2000

TRACK	AVERAGE SPEED, IN MILES (KM) PER HOUR	DRIVER
Michigan International Speedway	203 (327)	Marcos Ambrose
Daytona International Speedway	196 (315)	Danica Patrick
Texas Motor Speedway	196 (315)	Brian Vickers
Atlanta Motor Speedway	195 (314)	Ryan Newman
Charlotte Motor Speedway	193 (311)	Elliott Sadler
Talladega Superspeedway	192 (309)	David Gilliland
Kansas Speedway	191 (307)	Kasey Kahne

DANICA PATRICK

WHAT A DRAG!

There are fascinating statistics for all race cars. But few would argue that some of the most shocking and incredible stats involve dragsters. Judge for yourself.

Acceleration. A Top Fuel car can go from 0 to 100 miles (0 to 161 km) per hour in less than one second. That's faster than a fighter jet!

Fastest Funny Car. Matt Hagan set the Funny Car speed record in a 2016 race in Topeka, Kansas, with a speed of 335.57 miles (540 km) per hour.

Fastest Top Fuel. In a 2015 race in Brainerd, Minnesota, Spencer Massey set the Top Fuel speed record at 332.75 miles (535.51 km) per hour.

Force. Top Fuel cars blast off the starting line with the same force as a space shuttle launch!

Gallons per mile. How much gas a regular car burns is measured by how many miles it can travel on a gallon of gas, or miles per gallon. Top Fuel and Funny Car engines are measured in *gallons per mile*. They burn more than 4 gallons (15 liters) of gas on a 1,000-foot (305 m) track. That's more than 16 gallons (61 liters) per mile (1.6 km).

Power. A Top Fuel car has eight cylinders that power its engine. Just one of those cylinders produces 1,250 **horsepower**. That's more horsepower than all eight of the cylinders in a NASCAR engine can produce together.

FUNNY CAR

BUILDING A WINNER

Formula One has 10 teams with two cars each. Each team has designers, engineers, and other specialists. These workers are called constructors. Constructors represent companies such as Ferrari that made the car's main parts. Constructors assemble the parts into a working race car. A huge amount of money and time goes into designing, building, and testing F1 cars.

A FERRARI
FORMULA ONE CAR

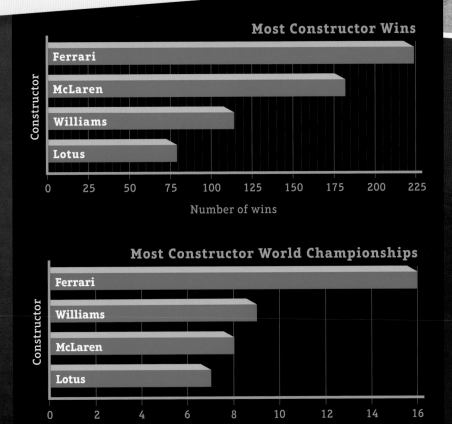

Most Constructor Wins

Constructor	Number of wins
Ferrari	225
McLaren	180
Williams	113
Lotus	79

Number of wins: 0, 25, 50, 75, 100, 125, 150, 175, 200, 225

Most Constructor World Championships

Constructor	Number of championships
Ferrari	16
Williams	9
McLaren	8
Lotus	7

Number of championships: 0, 2, 4, 6, 8, 10, 12, 14, 16

THAT'S THE PITS

Cars wear out their tires and burn fuel as they race. New tires and more fuel are the main reasons for a pit stop. The driver enters pit road and pulls into his team's pit box. The pit crew springs into action. Every second counts. The race doesn't pause for pit stops, so crews scramble to get the car back on the track as quickly as possible. How fast they do it is a pit crew's most important statistic. In NASCAR a 12-second pit stop is fast.

PIT STOP

TIME AT A PIT STOP

0.5 seconds. The pit crew hops over the wall as the car arrives in the pit box.

2 seconds. A worker raises the right side of the car with a jack. Another crew member inserts two gas can nozzles into the fuel tank.

4 seconds. Tire changers remove each wheel's five lug nuts on the right side of the car. Crew members remove the worn-out tires.

6 seconds. Crew members mount new tires on the car. The tire changers add the lug nuts. A crew member lowers the right side of the car.

8 seconds. The crew moves to the left side of the car.

10 seconds. They raise the car and remove the lug nuts. The tire changers remove the worn-out tires.

12 seconds. The crew mounts new tires and adds the lug nuts. They lower the left side, and the driver takes off to rejoin the race.

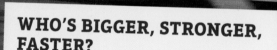

NASCAR

WHO'S BIGGER, STRONGER, FASTER?

Top Fuel and Funny Car races are a blaze of action for a few seconds—and then they're over. But NASCAR, IndyCar, and F1 races go on for hours before a winner crosses the finish line. These three types of race cars don't look alike, but how different are they really?

STATS FACT

A Formula One car's steering wheel costs about $45,000.

CAR	TOP SPEED, IN MILES (KM) PER HOUR	ENGINE HORSEPOWER	WEIGHT, IN POUNDS (KG)	COST*
Formula One	220 (354)	750	1,415 (642)	$400 million
IndyCar	240 (386)	550–700	1,565 (710)	$8 million
NASCAR	220 (354)	850	3,350 (1,520)	$15–20 million

*Cost includes design and construction of the car.

CHAPTER THREE

STATS ARE HERE TO STAY

THE LEADERBOARD

The earliest auto races were often held on 1-mile (1.6 km) dirt tracks built for horse racing. Much has changed since then. But the way fans read stats is just about the same. Race results appear on a leaderboard. The leaderboard shows some of the important elements of a race. You could write an entire story about a race by looking at this chart full of numbers. But first, you need to know what the words and numbers mean. Refer to the key on the next page to study the box score.

2016 DAYTONA 500

2016
DAYTONA 500

Key

Pos	= finishing position
Driver	= race car driver
Car	= race car number
Maker	= maker of car's main parts
Laps	= number of laps completed
Start	= position at start of race
Led	= number of laps spent in the lead

2016 Daytona 500

Pos	Driver	Car	Maker	Laps	Start	Led
1	Denny Hamlin	11	Toyota	200	11	95
2	Martin Truex Jr.	78	Toyota	200	28	2
3	Kyle Busch	18	Toyota	200	4	19
4	Kevin Harvick	4	Chevrolet	200	9	0
5	Carl Edwards	19	Toyota	200	10	0
6	Joey Logano	22	Ford	200	5	0
7	Kyle Larson	42	Chevrolet	200	14	0
8	Regan Smith	7	Chevrolet	200	27	0
9	Austin Dillon	3	Chevrolet	200	21	1
10	Kurt Busch	41	Chevrolet	200	8	0
11	Ryan Newman	31	Chevrolet	200	38	1
12	Aric Almirola	43	Ford	200	34	0
13	Kasey Kahne	5	Chevrolet	200	13	0
14	Matt Kenseth	20	Toyota	200	2	40
15	Michael McDowell	59	Chevrolet	200	39	0
16	Jimmie Johnson	48	Chevrolet	200	26	18
17	Jamie McMurray	1	Chevrolet	200	6	0
18	Paul Menard	27	Chevrolet	200	37	0
19	Ryan Blaney	21	Ford	200	7	0
20	Brad Keselowski	2	Ford	200	25	1

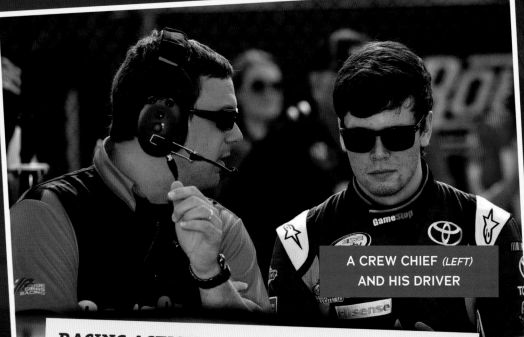

A CREW CHIEF *(LEFT)*
AND HIS DRIVER

RACING ACTION

Fans love to read about the stats of their favorite cars and drivers. Car designers and mechanics also examine the numbers. Constructors build cars to be as fast and safe as possible. They watch a car's statistics closely and look for ways to improve its performance.

A race car's average speed varies from track to track and race to race. Crew chiefs and drivers consider the numbers as they make decisions during races. For instance, a car that has fallen behind on a twisty track may have to take risks to catch up, such as speeding around dangerous corners faster than usual. The pit crew compares the average speed of their car to the average speed of the other racers. The crew calculates how much faster their car needs to go to catch up while still staying safe.

FANTASY AND THE FUTURE

Adult auto racing fans may play a game called fantasy racing. Fantasy racing uses the real statistics of drivers. Fantasy players, called owners, choose drivers to form teams. Fantasy owners win or lose based on the stats of the drivers on their team. Owners can usually add or drop drivers and make trades with other owners. One study showed that 56.8 million people in the United States and Canada played fantasy sports in 2015.

As the popularity of stats grows, crew chiefs study the numbers more than ever. And there are a lot more numbers to study. Modern race cars and drivers are dotted with **sensors**. The devices monitor the tires, the fuel, and many other parts of the car. They also record every movement the driver makes. The more stats auto racing teams can study, the better decisions they can make. It will be fun to see how statistics will affect racing in the future.

STATS MATCHUP

Jimmie Johnson and Kevin Harvick are two of NASCAR's top drivers. Fans love to compare their statistics and argue about which driver is better. Harvick joined NASCAR in 2001, and Johnson started a year later.

Jimmie Johnson	
Wins	79
Career top-five finishes	217
2015 top-five finishes	14
2016 top-five finishes	10
Career top-ten finishes	329
2015 top-ten finishes	22
2016 top-ten finishes	15

JIMMIE JOHNSON

Compare their Cup Series statistics since 2003. Who do you think is the best driver in NASCAR's top level? Johnson has the overall advantage in stats. But in recent years, Harvick has finished more races in the top five or top ten than Johnson has.

KEVIN HARVICK

Kevin Harvick	
Wins	35
Career top-five finishes	153
2015 top-five finishes	23
2016 top-five finishes	16
Career top-ten finishes	282
2015 top-ten finishes	28
2016 top-ten finishes	26

GLOSSARY

Cup Series: NASCAR's racing series that includes the biggest races and the most prize money

dirt tracks: racetracks with a clay or dirt surface rather than the more common asphalt surface

horsepower: a unit that tracks the power of an engine

medium tracks: oval tracks that are 1 to 2 miles (1.6 to 3.2 km) long

open-wheel: a car with its wheels outside the main body of the car

pit stops: quick stops in areas just off the track where a crew refuels a car and changes its tires

qualifying lap: one complete lap around a track to determine the starting positions for a race. The fastest cars begin the race at the head of the pack.

road courses: tracks that feature left- and right-hand turns, rather than oval courses, which have only left-hand turns. They are also called street courses.

sensors: devices that measure and record a physical property such as heat or movement

short tracks: oval tracks that are less than 1 mile (1.6 km) long

speedways: tracks that are greater than 2 miles (3.2 km) long. These are also called superspeedways.

stock cars: race cars that look like cars you see on the street

victory lane: an area where a race's winner goes to receive the trophy. Victory lane is also called the winner's circle.

FURTHER INFORMATION

Championship NHRA Drag Racing
http://www.nhra.com

Formula One
http://www.formula1.com

IndyCar Stats
http://www.indycar.com/Stats

NASCAR
http://www.nascar.com

Roe Pimm, Nancy. *The Daytona 500: The Thrill and Thunder of the Great American Race*. Minneapolis: Millbrook Press, 2011.

Scarpati, Kevin. *Indianapolis 500*. La Jolla, CA: Scobre Educational, 2015.

INDEX

PHOTO ACKNOWLEDGMENTS

The images in this book are used with the permission of: background: © iStockphoto.com/nycshooter; bar graphs: Laura Westlund/Independent Picture Service; © iStockphoto.com/peepo, p. 1; David J. Griffin/Icon Sportswire/Newscom, pp. 4, 28–32 (background); AP Photo/Icon Sportswire/Michael Allo, p. 5 (top); AP Photo/Icon Sportswire/Larry Placido, p. 5 (bottom); AP Photo/Brian Horton, p. 6; AP Photo/Russell LaBounty/NKP, p. 8; AP Photo/Terry Renna, pp. 9, 23; © Dozier Mobley/Getty Images, p. 10; AP Photo/Icon Sportswire/Dan Sanger, p. 11; AP Photo/Mel Evans, p. 13; AP Photo/Pascal Rondequ/Sipa USA, p. 15; AP Photo/Jeff Speer/Icon Sportswire, p. 16; AP Photo/Mark Almond, p. 19; AP Photo/Michael Allio/Icon Sportswire, p. 20; AP Photo/Vincent Thian, p. 21; AP Photo/Ralph Freso, p. 22; AP Photo/Nigel Kinrade/NKP, p. 24; AP Photo/Wilfredo Lee, p. 25; AP Photo/NKP/Logan Whitton, p. 26; AP Photo/Sephan Savovia, p. 27; © Rey Del Rio/Getty Images, pp. 28, 29.

Cover: © iStockphoto.com/peepo (race car).

Back cover: © iStockphoto.com/nycshooter (racetrack).